**SPECIAL OLYMPICS**

# SPECIAL OLYMPICS

BY FERN G. BROWN

Franklin Watts
New York   London   Toronto   Sydney
A First Book

Cover photographs copyright © : Special Olympics International, Washington, D.C. / Ken Regan / Camera 5

Photographs copyright © : Special Olympics International, Washington, D.C.: pp. 2, 16 top, 16 bottom (Leet-Melbrook), 22, 29, 57 bottom (all Ken Regan / Camera 5), 18, 26 bottom, 38, 41 bottom, 48, 51 top, 57 top; Kansas Special Olympics, Mission, KS.: pp. 26 top, 31; All-Sport USA / Scott Halleran: p. 35; New Trier High School / Lew Goldstein: p. 41 top; Louisiana State University: pp. 46, 53 (both Jim Zietz), 51 bottom (Prather Warren).

Library of Congress Cataloging-in-Publication Data

Brown, Fern G.
Special Olympics / Fern G. Brown.
p. cm. — (A first book)
Includes index.
Summary: Describes the history and organization of the Special Olympics and explains how athletes and volunteers can get involved.
ISBN 0-531-20062-0
1. Special Olympics — Juvenile literature. [1. Special Olympics.] I. Title. II. Series.
GV722.5.S64B76 1992
796'.0196 — dc20                                                91-31661 CIP AC

Copyright © 1992 Fern G. Brown
All rights reserved
Printed in the United States of America
6 5 4 3

# CONTENTS

Introduction
11

**1**
The Beginning of
Special Olympics
13

**2**
How Special
Olympics Works
21

**3**
Volunteers
33

**4**
You Had
to Be There!
44

**5**
Future Goals
55

Glossary
59

Index
62

This book is dedicated to
the Special Olympics athletes who
try hard, achieve so much, and live
by the Special Olympics oath:
Let me win.
But if I cannot win,
let me be brave
in the attempt.

# ACKNOWLEDGMENTS

The author and editors wish to express their appreciation to the following for their assistance in the preparation of this book:

Illinois Special Olympics: Sandy Hutchins, Northeastern Area Director, and Amy Kaylor.

Texas Special Olympics: Karen Siegel, Program Director of Management and Training.

New York Special Olympics: Diane Shuger, Assistant Executive Director, and Debra Rausch, Director of Public Information and Communications.

Colorado Special Olympics: Nancy Sawyer, Communications.

Special Olympics International: Lari Johnson, Julie Borchard, and Andrea Cahn, Communications Department.

Thank you to Lewis Goldstein, teacher at New Trier High School, Winnetka, Illinois, and everyone in his unique EMH program for their splendid cooperation.

A very special thank you to Dick Strauss, Illinois Special Olympics State Aquatics Director, whose enthusiasm for Special Olympics provided the force behind this book, and to Anne McGlone Burke for her wonderful cooperation.

# INTRODUCTION

All over the world, superior athletes are treated like "Very Important Persons." We all admire and look up to them. For many years a person with **mental retardation** didn't stand a chance of being an athletic V.I.P. But now things have changed. Through Special Olympics, individuals with mental retardation are given the opportunity to participate in organized athletics. Children and adults of all ages and ability levels are offered year-round training and athletic competition in twenty-two well-coached Olympic-type summer and winter sports. It's the fastest growing sports program in the world.

Special Olympics athletes are challenged to test their limits. Those who take up the challenge, besides building their self-confidence and skills, meet other Special Olympians with similar goals. Pulling for the team carries over into their lives at school, at home, and at work.

In order for Special Olympics athletes to be good at what they do and build up their bodies, they must work hard. A great deal of time and energy is spent practicing. Of course, they try to win. But winning isn't what it's all about. The idea is to give one's best effort and enjoy the competition. Participating is a victory too—not only for the athletes, but for their entire families.

Everyone wins in Special Olympics. Let's find out what it takes to be a player on the Special Olympics team.

## CHAPTER ONE
## THE BEGINNING OF SPECIAL OLYMPICS

Jerilyn was almost forty when she became pregnant. The doctor told her it was risky to have a first baby at her age, but she and her husband had been wanting a child for so long that they shrugged off his warnings. Their son, Frank, Jr., was born with **Down syndrome** and had mental retardation. Yet Jerilyn and Frank didn't love him any less because he had problems. "Frankie is a very special kid," Jerilyn said. "If I never had a child, that would have been really sad."

According to Special Olympics International, 300 million people in the world have mental retardation. Seven million live in the United States, and about 100,000 mentally retarded babies are born in the United States each year.

For various reasons, people with mental retardation are limited in their ability to think and understand. They have short attention spans and may learn at a much slower pace than the average person of the same age. Yet many of them have relatively good memories and they can and do learn.

## HOW SPECIAL OLYMPICS BEGAN

Mrs. Eunice Kennedy Shriver has been a leader in trying to improve the lives of people with mental retardation since 1957 when she became the director of the Joseph P. Kennedy, Jr., Foundation. The foundation was established in 1946 as a memorial to the eldest Kennedy son, who was killed in World War II. Its purpose was to prevent mental retardation by finding its causes, and to find better ways to deal with those who have mental retardation. Mrs. Shriver's sister Rosemary, now in her seventies, was born with mental retardation.

In the early 1960s a friend asked Mrs. Shriver to suggest a summer camp for a person with mental retardation. When Mrs. Shriver found there was no such camp, she became angry. Where were retarded people supposed to go to have fun and enjoy sports? She resolved to do something about it. In June 1963, she and her husband, Sargent Shriver, started a five-week day camp in their large backyard in Rockville, Maryland. There were one hundred **volunteers**—one for each camper that summer. The campers rode horses, learned to swim, played tennis and volleyball, did gymnastics, and shot bows and arrows. All the sports were adapted to meet their mental and physical capabilities.

When camp was over, the Shrivers saw how much the campers' skills had improved. With proper instruction and plenty of encouragement they had done well in individual sports. As for team sports, they were every bit as competitive as anyone who had ever thrown a baseball. Mrs. Shriver began thinking about holding an event so trained athletes with mental retardation could compete in Olympic sports.

It so happened that in January of 1968, Anne McGlone and representatives of the Chicago Park District asked the Kennedy Foundation to help fund a national Olympic event for children with mental retardation. It was just what Mrs. Shriver was thinking about. If these individuals could participate in a Special Olympics, she said, it would help them win respect at home and in their communities. The Chicagoans also felt that peo-

In 1963 Camp Shriver allowed people with mental retardation to enjoy athletics and have fun.

ple with mental retardation deserved a chance to give Olympic sports their best shot.

They were given that chance at the first Special Olympics Summer Games, modeled after the traditional Olympic Games. Co-sponsored by the Chicago Park District and the Kennedy Foundation, the Games were held on July 20, 1968, at Soldier Field in Chicago, Illinois. Almost 1,000 people with mental retardation from twenty-six U.S. states and Canada competed in track and field and swimming events.

Everyone was so pleased with the games that the next year a nonprofit corporation was established called Special Olympics Incorporated. By 1970, all fifty states, the District of Columbia, and Canada had Special Olympics chapters.

Each year the number of Special Olympics programs kept increasing. In 1983, at the Sixth International Summer Special Olympics Games at Louisiana State University, four thousand athletes representing all fifty U.S. states and fifty other countries participated. The event made the ABC "Wide World of Sports" broadcast.

Special Olympics Winter Games were added with competition in skiing and skating events. And European Special Olympics Games were also being held. At the second European Special Olym-

Athletes from Iceland march
into the opening ceremonies.

pics Games in Dublin, Ireland, in July 1985, two thousand athletes from eighteen countries competed. It was heartwarming to see athletes from Northern and Southern Ireland, parts of the island that had been fighting one another for years, marching together. That same year, the People's Republic of China became the sixty-fifth nation to join Special Olympics International.

In 1988, Special Olympics celebrated its twentieth anniversary with programs in every U.S. state, four U.S. territories, and seventy-three countries. Training and competition was offered in ten summer sports, six winter sports, and six demonstration sports. Today, with an annual budget of $10.5 million, there are accredited Special Olympics programs in nearly one hundred countries, and programs are being developed in more than twenty other nations. It was a giant step forward for mental retardation when on February 15, 1988, Special Olympics was officially recognized and endorsed by the International Olympic Committee.

The third European Special Olympics Games were held in Strathclyde, Scotland, in July 1990. They were the largest European games in the history of Special Olympics International. It was especially exciting because athletes from Czechoslovakia, Estonia, Hungary, Iceland, Latvia, Lithuania, and the USSR participated for the first time.

In 1991 the Eighth International Summer Games were held in Minneapolis-St. Paul, Minnesota, with six thousand athletes from more than ninety countries. Special Olympics had come a long way from its first summer games at Soldier Field in Chicago.

## CHAPTER TWO
## HOW SPECIAL OLYMPICS WORKS

Connie Lynn Roll, a young woman of nineteen, has mental retardation and **cerebral palsy.** Connie wanted to swim in competition but because she was confined to a wheelchair most of the time, she wondered if she could join Special Olympics. Connie was accepted into a swimming program.

All people with mental retardation from the ages of eight up, regardless of their ability or whether they are physically **disabled**, are eligible for Special Olympics. Male or female, white, black, yellow, or brown, rich or poor, wherever they live, everyone is welcome. But they must have a doctor's permission.

### SPECIAL OLYMPICS INTERNATIONAL NETWORK

Special Olympics International is headquartered in Washington, D.C. It maintains an international

Special Olympics athletes with physical disabilities are also eligible to compete in events.

network of programs through which information and new ideas are exchanged. The governing body, a volunteer board of directors, is made up of people from more than thirty-five countries.

Directors of Regional Development throughout the world assist their country's programs and help start new programs.

Every National Special Olympics Program is administered by a director selected by a national committee. This committee is the governing body of Special Olympics in that country. National and local Special Olympics groups receive donations from sources such as individuals, foundations, and corporations.

## WAYS TO BECOME A SPECIAL OLYMPICS ATHLETE

Elsie Okitkon, an Inupiouq Eskimo teenager, lives in the tiny rural village of Koyuk, Alaska; population, 225. Although Elsie had been skiing since she was five, she had not entered into competition because she was terribly shy. Being different in such a small community made her stand out. Then at school she heard about Special Olympics. Elsie began competing in local competitions—and winning. She was chosen to be on the Alaskan team that went to the 1989 International Winter Games in Reno, Nevada. Because of Special Olympics, Elsie came out of her shell and became a local celebrity.

There are Special Olympics programs in nearly every community in the United States. The two main ways to join Special Olympics are through school and through the recommendation of local park district directors. Athletes may also join through sports and civic groups, religious organizations, and places where they work. One woman joined Special Olympics because she saw how much her neighbor's daughter had accomplished in the program. Special Olympics athletes and their families are often the best advertisements for Special Olympics.

Special Olympics provides training to prepare and certify coaches. It sets up rules, and coordinates the games. Besides teaching skills, coaches encourage the athletes to do their best.

"Marty" (Martha) Drake, a physical education teacher at New Trier High School in Winnetka, Illinois, is a volunteer Special Olympics coach. She has taken training in sports such as track and field and **poly hockey** at Special Olympics coaching clinics in various parts of the state. She also attends rules meetings and keeps up on the latest news through the Special Olympics newsletter.

Official Special Olympics sports follow international rules with minor adaptations depending on the needs of the athletes. Because the proper instruction is so important, athlete training programs are outlined in a "Sports Skills Guide" to each sport. Every person with mental retardation, no matter how severe, can find an activity to fit his or her physical and mental ability.

Special Olympics isn't only a once-a-year or once-every-two-years competition. Special Olympics athletes work all year around with their coaches, and local competitions are held frequently. In the United States, Special Olympics programs take place in 25,000 areas and districts. In order that they have a fair chance to win a medal, the participants are grouped according to age, sex, and past scores or times, into divisions with others who are within approximately 10 percent of their ability. After athletes qualify in local competition, they are eligible to compete in state and international games.

National programs hold games annually or biennially. International games are held every two years, alternating between winter and summer sports.

At the International Games awards ceremo-

nies you won't hear the "Star Spangled Banner" or any other national anthem. Medals are not given to the country the athlete is from. In Special Olympics it is the individual's effort and achievement that counts.

In addition to the gold, silver, and bronze medals for first, second, and third places, respectively, athletes who finish from fourth to last are given ribbons. Those who place last get the same respect and applause from friends and family as do the gold medal winners.

Many people with mental retardation are excellent athletes. Their Special Olympics training gives them the skills and confidence they need to participate in school and community sports events open to all.

(Top) Although there is no snow, this clinic trains athletes in Nordic cross-country skiing. (Bottom) All the athletes who compete in Special Olympics are awarded medals or ribbons—and all are pleased with the recognition they received.

# MODEL PROGRAMS

**Model School District Programs** have been set up by U.S. chapters to involve elementary and high school students with mental retardation in **extra-curricular** and **interscholastic** sports. Another aim of the model programs is to include Special Olympics in the physical education curriculum.

**Model Community Programs** coordinate Special Olympics training and competition in schools, community programs, group homes, and institutions.

## UNIFIED SPORTS

Special Olympians often become skilled enough in a sport to compete with **non-handicapped peers.** A good example is the Texas softball team that has both athletes with mental retardation and those without on the same team. This is called **Unified Sports** and is Special Olympics' fastest growing new program. The Texas team plays in a regular community softball league, and it has more fans than any other team. In some schools and communities there are whole leagues of unified sports, and unified sports teams now compete at Special Olympics Games.

Unified Sports is one of Special Olympics' fastest-growing programs. This unified softball team celebrates a victory.

## MOTOR ACTIVITIES TRAINING PROGRAM (MATP)

This program began in 1989 to provide motor activity and recreation training for those with severe mental retardation or multiple handicaps. These individuals compete at a lower level of physical ability.

Using a special program guide, MATP coaches provide individually suited activities for each participant. Then after a training period of at least eight weeks, those in the program may take part in a Special Olympics Training Day. One young man who took part in such a training day showed his best by simply throwing a tennis ball. He was applauded for the accomplishment as heartily as if he had pitched a shutout in the World Series. His ear-to-ear smile showed he was having fun and enjoyed being part of Special Olympics. That is what this program is trying to accomplish. Its goal is not always to prepare the participants to compete in a sport. Yet many in the MATP do gain the skills to compete in certain Special Olympics sports events.

## SPECIAL OLYMPICS SPORTS

Each chapter selects its sports from a list of twenty-two sports approved by Special Olympics

Athletes stand ready for action at a state floor hockey tournament in Kansas.

International. The official summer sports are aquatics, athletics, basketball, bowling, horseback riding, gymnastics, roller skating, soccer, softball, and volleyball. The official winter sports are alpine skiing, cross-country skiing, figure skating, speed-skating, floor hockey, and poly hockey, which is played indoors with a plastic stick and puck.

Mandy Meder of New Trier High School enjoys Special Olympics sports all year around. She won a silver medal in Frisbee™ and a bronze in softball last year. When she played offense on her high school poly-hockey team, they won a gold in an area meet. Although she weighs only 82 pounds, Mandy lifts weights up to 120 pounds. When asked how good she was at shooting baskets, she grinned, "You gotta see me in action, lady."

**Demonstration sports** such as canoeing, cycling, powerlifting, team handball, tennis, and table tennis are also included at official games. In addition, some areas offer other locally popular sports and demonstrate them at official games. Certain sports, such as **karate** and **javelin throw**, are not included because they could cause injury to the athletes.

## CHAPTER THREE
## VOLUNTEERS

It may be Special Olympics that provides the training and the rules, and organizes the games, but it's the volunteers at the community level that help make each event special and fill the games with spirit.

Dick Strauss is a Deerfield, Illinois, businessman whose youngest son once had major heart surgery. Dick was so grateful for the boy's recovery that he called the Illinois Special Olympics office and volunteered, as he put it, "to give something back." He is now a National Championship Certified Swimming and Diving Referee and a Nationally Certified Special Olympics swimming coach. His entire family has also become involved in Special Olympics. Dick's older sons are lifeguards at the meets; his wife, a referee, organizes the races; and his youngest son works on the deck. Even Dick's parents attend the events.

In Special Olympics there are over 500,000 volunteers, including 100,000 coaches, who are involved in the program worldwide—more volunteers than in any other sports organization. In the New York chapter, for example, from secretarial to management level, there are twenty-seven salaried people and 15,000 volunteers, making the chapter over 90 percent volunteer.

Volunteers come from schools and universities, civic organizations, government, private industry, athletic associations, and from the families of Special Olympics athletes.

Laura, Rebecca, and Sarah Zimmerman, Massachusetts teenagers, are triplets. Laura and Rebecca, who are identical twins, have Down syndrome and they train and compete in Special Olympics speed skating. Sarah, the third sister, who is not identical, is a Special Olympics volunteer.

A volunteer may be anyone from a young person to a senior citizen. Age makes little difference. There are so many places where volunteers are needed at the local, state, national, and international levels that there is a job for anyone who wants to help.

An athlete and a volunteer anxiously watch an event from the sidelines.

Sometimes Special Olympics athletes themselves volunteer to help other athletes. Jacob Asmussen, a Colorado teenager, is a fine Special Olympics skier. He competes in the **slalom** and giant slalom. School classmate Jenny McIntosh, who is in a wheelchair, is Jacob's **peer-buddy.** He pushes her chair at school, and she helps him with his studies. Jenny participated in the **assisted skiing events** last winter at the Colorado Special Olympics, and Jacob helped her get around.

Volunteers with expertise in a particular sport may serve as certified Special Olympics coaches during sports training or as certified officials or games directors at competitions. They may use their know-how to help set up clinics and demonstrate new sports. Volunteers may organize, coach, or play on Unified Sports teams, or work in the Special Olympics sports camps. They can also help train those with severe handicaps through the MATP.

The volunteers who work in administrative and clerical positions are important, too. They serve on boards of directors or area committees, provide services in legal or accounting departments, and donate computer skills. Many doctors give free physicals and medical support to the athletes. And there's also a need for volunteer photographers and people with public relations and writing skills.

At the Games, volunteers help with registration, serve as timers and scorers, give out awards, and sometimes help rotate the athletes to the various events. One Special Olympics athlete's father worked as a driver at the State Summer Games, his mother served food in the hospitality tent, and his sister was a cheerleader.

When a North Carolina Special Olympics volunteer was asked what her job was, she shrugged, "I'm nothing but a hugger—I give hugs and high fives at the finish line." But these volunteers are needed too. Special Olympics athletes would be terribly disappointed if they didn't find a smiling face waiting for them after each event.

Many civic groups have adopted a Special Olympics chapter or team, or have organized a combined team. Several clubs have gone on hikes and picnics with Special Olympics athletes or have worked as volunteers at a group home or institution.

Randy Berkhart, coach for Colorado's International Ski Team, has set up a year-round training program for Special Olympian Jacob Asmussen, and Jacob doesn't have to pay him a penny. No training or coaching fees are ever

It takes time and training for an athlete to reach this point—competition with others, and against himself.

charged Special Olympics athletes. There aren't any entrance fees at the Games for athletes or for spectators. As one coach put it, "My pay is the look of joy and pride on the face of each athlete."

A handbook is provided by Special Olympics to familiarize volunteers with athletes who have mental retardation and teach them how to carry on Special Olympics activities in their communities.

In order to become aquatics sports director of Illinois, Dick Strauss attended certified training sessions. Although he now runs training sessions himself for new volunteers, he still takes ten to twenty hours of training every year.

## HOW SCHOOLS CAN HELP

At New Trier High School, Lewis Goldstein teaches **Educable** Mentally Handicapped classes. The Special Olympics part of his unique EMH program began twelve years ago.

At her adviser's suggestion, Joey Kirschner, a junior at New Trier, volunteered as a student helper in the EMH program. "I love it a lot," she said. "I can be having the worst day and then I come in here and work. Well, I go out feeling great." She smiled shyly, "I'm a better person because of it. I've learned tolerance and patience."

Joey went to an area tournament recently with New Trier's Special Olympics poly-hockey team. "We worked very hard preparing for the Games. The athletes have tons of pride in what they do," she said. "They won a trophy and several medals, but just being there meant so much to them."

Erin Crowley, another student at New Trier, coached poly hockey and also volunteered at the Games. She explained that before she was involved in the program, she had many misconceptions about handicapped people, but getting to know them and making friends with them made her realize how capable they were. Now she and other student helpers go to school games with their special friends and cheer for the varsity teams.

Robert D'Egidio, one of Lewis Goldstein's former students, used to come late to Special Olympics practices because he was just not interested. "I thought it was more fun to watch sports on TV than to compete," he said. But Robert was persuaded to train for Special Olympics and he turned into a super athlete. Now he is attending junior college and has a job. But he still takes the

(Above) At New Trier High School in Winnetka, Illinois, many Special Olympics athletes and student volunteers have become friends through the Special Olympics program at the school.
(Left) Law enforcement officers work hard to raise money for Special Olympics. Here, they carry a torch as they run a marathon to earn the pledges sponsors have promised to Special Olympics.

time to come back to the gym and play poly hockey and other sports with his former schoolmates. "I'm a role model for these kids," Robert says proudly.

Schools can help those who are mentally handicapped by including Special Olympics sports training in the adapted physical education curriculum, as New Trier does, or by putting Special Olympics in their after-school sports programs. Schools could also start Special Olympics Unified Sports teams or Sports Partnerships. And members of their sports teams could become certified Special Olympics coaches.

The best way to help those with mental retardation would be to conduct Special Olympics training and competitions during a school's regular sports practices and events.

## VOLUNTEERS AS FUND-RAISERS

There are nearly one million competitors in Special Olympics each year. It costs $32.58 per athlete each season for the Special Olympics program, so there is always a need for money. Fund-raising campaigns are run by schools, churches, and civic organizations. Volunteer fund-raisers ask for donations from individuals and businesses. They use telephone campaigns to inform the public about Special Olympics and to get pledges of money for the Law Enforcement Torch Run, when police officers run a relay to raise money for Special Olympics.

Special Olympics volunteers have done a great deal for those with mental retardation, but as one volunteer put it, "My life has been enriched too. Whatever I've done it's not enough. I always want to know what else I can do."

## CHAPTER FOUR
## YOU HAD TO BE THERE!

At the Illinois Special Olympics Games in Bloomington, the crowd milled about in heat that sent the thermometer soaring. Yet no amount of heat could melt the triumphant smiles of the athletes or their families. Something special was going on.

The kickoff event, the lighting of the Olympic torch, took place in Redbird Arena. Athletes lined up to march into the arena. And march they did, waving banners, pom-poms, and flags, in a rainbow of T-shirts—the green of Woodson North, the red of Starved Rock, the blue and gold of Marquette, the yellow of Fairfield—just a sampling of the twenty-four areas participating.

They came with fast steps, slow steps, and somersaults. Some rolled their wheelchairs through the arch of blue and yellow balloons as the crowd cheered themselves hoarse.

A voice over the loudspeaker asked, "Are you having fun?" "YES!" shouted the athletes. "Are you proud of your achievements?" "YES!" responded the three thousand Illinois champions. "You are the best athletes in the state," the Special Olympians were told. "It took talent, training, and discipline for you to get here. If you win, it is true competition against yourself."

Holding a lighted torch high in the air, a police officer ran into the arena. He represented the law-enforcement men and women who carried the torch hundreds of miles, raising money for Special Olympics. The crowd stamped and whistled their approval as the flaming torch was passed to a Special Olympics athlete who ran around the arena, and then gave it to another athlete who circled and passed it on. This Special Olympics athlete took the torch up a flight of stairs to where another athlete was waiting. When this last athlete lit the Olympic flame, signaling the start of the Games, the spectators rose to their feet with a roar.

## THE STATE MEET

In order to advance to the state meet, these athletes had to win gold medals in regional competitions. The gold medal winners at the state meet

will then have their names put into nomination for the next International Games. For example, say there are forty-four slots for swimmers at the next International Games and there are sixty winners here. Winners' names will be submitted to the state office and forty-four athletes will be selected to represent their state program at the International Games.

In the gym, several events were going on at the same time. At one end, women athletes were competing in gymnastics on a large red mat. The last of six participants was poised to do the routine that she had practiced dozens of times. First she jumped in place, carefully moving her shoulders and neck, eyes glued on her coach. Then she performed a dance routine to the rhythm of recorded music and ended with a somersault. She rose with a satisfied smile and ran over for her two-hug reward—one from her younger sister and another from her coach. The little sister said, "I'm proud of her. I'm going to tell all the kids at school how good she did."

Men were performing on the balance beam and parallel bars. After doing his routine, one athlete jumped down and ran off with his hand waving in the air to give a high-five to his coach, teammates, and anyone else with a free right hand.

A gymnast concentrates on her routine, which she has practiced for many, many hours.

The next fellow bit his lip in concentration while he painstakingly did his routine. When he finished, he exclaimed, "I did it!" and covered his face with his hands. The athlete's father commented, "He feels really good about himself."

When it was time for the last participant, he came up and waved to his family. His mom and dad were in the bleachers all smiles, and their baby was asleep in a stroller. Suddenly the gym grew quiet. This athlete was attempting to do a more difficult routine on the parallel bars. Slowly, very slowly, he went through his movements. Everyone held their breath, silently cheering him on. When he finished, his coach yelled, "Yeah!" above the thunderous applause. The gymnast smiled, stuck out his chest, and put two thumbs up. How proud he was! Someone jumped in front with a camera and snapped his picture.

## THE SWIMMING POOL

A six-lane indoor swimming pool was the site of the swimming and diving matches. Swimming is a very popular sport here. The announcer called the names in each of the lanes, and then a whistle blew shrilly.

"They're off!" screamed the spectators.

Arms and legs churned the water, and the

crowd went wild cheering them on. "Go! Go! You can do it!" the words bounced off the walls and echoed around the humid room.

Not everything went smoothly, though. During a relay race both teams jumped into the pool before the electronic tone signal. But it didn't matter. They climbed out, and after a short rest started the event over again.

Connie Roll is a good swimmer and competitor. She doesn't let her cerebral palsy keep her from winning medals in the 50-meter freestyle. Speaking slowly she said how much she loved to swim because "it's good for you, and you feel great after you do it." She practices often at the YMCA with friends who swim. At first Connie said it didn't matter too much whether she wins or not, but then she smiled shyly and said, "I do want to win." About her coach, Dick Strauss, she said, "Dick helps me. I like him. He always comes over and hugs me."

## TRACK MEET

At the track meet, Steve showed off the bronze he had won in the standing long jump. "Look!" he said, "Isn't this a great medal?" Steve has been a participant in Special Olympics for years and always looks forward to coming to the games. "I

(Above) A swimmer is captured mid-breath at the 1991 summer games in Minneapolis-St. Paul. (Left) Competing is exciting enough, but winning—as is true for any athlete—makes the training even more worthwhile.

used to be lonely and scared, and other kids picked on me, but not now," he said. "I've got lots of friends and it's great to know people care about me."

A walking meet was going on. The athletes showed how well they could walk to the finish line, some with helpers. A hot wind blew across the track, and several spectators went for the shade of a nearby tent. But the participants didn't seem to mind the heat. When the cheers rang out, "Go get 'em, Billy," and "Way to go, Andy!" they grinned and flashed the victory sign.

## THE MIDWAY

Athletes waiting for their next event were invited to the midway. There were plenty of cold drinks, delicious snacks, and exciting carnival games. Athletes could burst a balloon with a dart, toss a cotton ball at a clown face, or put a hoop on moose antlers, and win a prize. Everything was free; the only thing you had to pay for were souvenirs.

## SOCCER GAME

Most Special Olympics activities were single events, but there were team games too. You could hop a shuttle bus to a soccer field and watch a

Soccer—a popular game all over the world—is played with passion at Special Olympics summer games.

game in action. The co-ed soccer teams did a fine job of keeping the ball going. They kicked and passed and tried their best to score a goal. "Good game!" everyone said when it was over and the winners were announced. The teams shook hands and all posed for a group picture.

When the meet ended, the Olympic torch was put out and it was time to think about what had been achieved in the last few days. The athletes had trained hard to become fit and ready to compete. They had been challenged to do their best, and had shown great inner strength and courage meeting that challenge.

Many new friendships had been formed with other Special Olympics athletes and their families, coaches, and volunteers. When the good-byes were said, there was a warm feeling of accomplishment and everyone talked about the state games to be held the following year.

One coach yelled, "How does everybody feel now?" A great big "OKAY!" split the air.

"Give yourselves a big hand!"

The applause could have been heard miles away in Chicago.

## CHAPTER FIVE
## FUTURE GOALS

Much has been accomplished in Special Olympics. It is something to celebrate when approximately one million children and adults with mental retardation in nearly one hundred nations participate in year-round athletic training and competitive events.

At the first International Summer Special Olympics Games fewer than 1,000 athletes with mental retardation from twenty-six states and Canada competed in two events. Twenty-three years later, in July 1991, the eighth International Summer Special Olympics Games, held in Minneapolis-St. Paul, Minnesota, was the largest sporting event held in the world that year. Some 6,000 athletes representing ninety-four countries competed in sixteen Special Olympics sports.

The name of the international games will be changed to World Games in 1993. That year, the fifth International Winter Games will be played in Schladming, Austria, where 1,500 athletes from over thirty-five countries are expected to compete.

By fighting discrimination against individuals with mental retardation with the largest amateur sports program in the world, Special Olympics has affected many lives. Not only has it helped the public to understand the emotional, physical, and social needs of people with mental retardation and their families, but it has done much to give hope to the 300 million people in the world with mental retardation. They see what the athletes have done, and they know that through Special Olympics they have the opportunity to do the same. While a great deal has been accomplished, there is still much to be done.

## HOW YOU CAN HELP

Urge those with mental retardation to become involved with a Special Olympics program. Make friends with them and invite them to join your community sports teams. Volunteer for a job in

(Left) A figure skater makes a turn at the 1989 International Winter Special Olympics. (Below) Competing in Special Olympics has made many athletes rightfully proud of what they can accomplish.

Special Olympics. Perhaps you can give time at your local ski area, skating rink, or bowling alley for Special Olympics practice sessions. If you belong to a club or service organization, get the members to help. The more volunteers, the better.

If you want to join Special Olympics, look in the phone book to locate the nearest office. To start a local or national program where none exists, write to Mrs. Eunice Kennedy Shriver, Special Olympics International, 1350 New York Avenue NW, Suite 500, Washington, D.C., 20005. If you are already a Special Olympics athlete, spread the word to others about the program. You can be a role model for new Special Olympics athletes.

A woman at one of the games wore a pin that seemed to sum it all up. It said, "Special Olympics athletes are neat people." So are their families, the coaches, and the other volunteers that do so much. So are the staff, administrators, and sponsors who give their time and energy to an exciting international movement that is truly uniting the world.

# GLOSSARY

**Assisted skiing event**—when a person competes in a skiing event with an adapted device.
**Cerebral palsy**—a decrease in the strength of muscular power and coordination due to brain damage usually at or before birth.
**Demonstration sports**—usually locally popular sports, but not included on the Special Olympics official list of sports.
**Disabled**—when usual physical or mental powers are weakened or destroyed.
**Down syndrome**—a birth disorder marked by some degree of mental retardation, and often a short flattened skull and slanted eyes.
**Educable**—capable of learning and being educated.
**Extracurricular**—outside the regular courses offered by a school.

**Interscholastic**—existing or conducted between or among schools.

**Javelin throw**—a contest to see how far a metal or metal-tipped spear, usually at least 8½ feet (2.5 m) long, can be thrown.

**Karate**—a Japanese art of self-defense, in which sharp blows and kicks are delivered to pressure-sensitive points on an opponent's body.

**Mental retardation**—a limitation in thinking and understanding, often accompanied by a short attention span. Those who have it may learn at a slower pace than the average individual of the same age, yet many have relatively good memories and a definite ability to learn.

**Model Community Program**—coordinates Special Olympics training and competition in schools, communities, group homes, and institutions.

**Model School District Program**—programs in U.S. chapters designed to involve elementary and high school students with mental retardation in extracurricular and interscholastic sports.

**Non-handicapped peers**—persons of comparable age or grade who do not have mental retardation.

**Peer-buddy**—one who assists a companion and in return gets help from that person in other ways.

**Poly hockey**—a game similar to field hockey, except played indoors with a plastic stick and puck.

**Slalom**—a ski race along a zigzagged course, laid out with flag-marked poles.

**Unified Sports**—a sports team made up of both athletes with mental retardation and those without it.

**Volunteer**—one who serves or helps of his or her own free will, and, in the case of the Special Olympics, without pay.

# INDEX

Page references in *italics* refer to illustrations.

Asmussen, Jacob, 36, 37

Berkhart, Randy, 37

Camp Shriver, 14–15, *16*
Chicago Park District, 15–17
Coaches, 24–25, 34, 36, 42
Crowley, Erin, 40

D'Egidio, Robert, 40–42
Demonstration sports, 32
Directors of Regional Development, 23
Drake, "Marty" (Martha), 24–25

Educable Mentally Handicapped classes (EMH), 39
European Special Olympics Games, 17–20

Floor hockey, *29*

Goldstein, Lewis, 39, 40
Gymnastics, 47–49, *48*

Illinois Special Olympics Games, 44–54
International Olympic Committee, 19
International Special Olympics Games, 17–20, 24, 25–27, 47, 55–56, 57

Joseph P. Kennedy, Jr., Foundation, 14, 15, 17
Kennedy, Rosemary, 14
Kirschner, Joey, 39–40

Law Enforcement Torch Run, *41*, 43, 45

McGlone, Anne, 15
McIntosh, Jenny, 36
Meder, Mandy, 32

Model Community Programs, 28
Model School District Programs, 27–28
Motor Activities Training Program (MATP), 28–30, 36

National committees, 23
New Trier High School, 39–42, *41*
Nordic cross-country skiing, *26*, 32

Okitkon, Elsie, 23–24

Peer-buddies, 36

Roll, Connie Lynn, 21, 50

Shriver, Eunice Kennedy, 14–15, 58
Shriver, Sargent, 15
Skating, 17, 34, *57*

Skiing, 17, 23–24, *26*, 36
Soccer, 52–54, *53*
Softball, 28, *29*
Special Olympics:
    administration of, 21–23
    awards for, 25–27, *26*
    beginning of, 14–17
    eligibility for, 21, 22
    fund-raising for, 23, *41*, 42–43
    future goals of, 55–58
    joining, 24
    opening ceremonies for, *18*, 44–45, *46*
    schools' help with, 39–42
    sports in, 30–32
Special Olympics International, 17, 21–23, 58
Special Olympics Training Day, 30
Sports Partnerships, 42
Strauss, Dick, 33–34, 39, 50
Swimming, 17, 21, 47, 49–50, *51*

Track and field, 17, 50–52

Unified Sports, 28, *29*, 36, 42

Volunteers, 33–43, *35*, *41*, 56–58
    as fund-raisers, *41*, 42–43
    jobs for, 36–37
    training of, 39

Walking meets, 52
"Wide World of Sports," 17
World Games, 56

Zimmerman sisters, 34